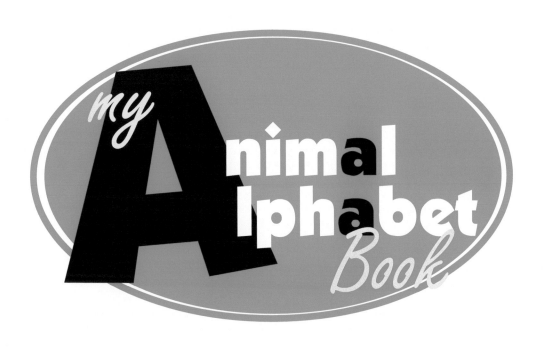

my Animal Alphabet Book

To order additional copies of this book, contact:
Xlibris
1-888-795-4274
www.Xlibris.com
Orders@Xlibris.com

my Animal Alphabet Book

And a Note to Parents
Who Want Their Children
to Succeed

DELORES
HENRIQUES

Aa

A is for Alligator.
Alligators live in ponds and lakes. They eat fish, birds and other animals. They build nests and lay their eggs. Out of each egg comes a baby alligator.

Bb

B is for Beaver.
Beavers are large rodents that like to live where there is water. They use sticks, branches and mud to build their homes on the banks of rivers and lakes. Their homes are called lodges.

Cc

C is for cat.
Cats are friendly animals. They make very good pets. They love to climb trees. The babies are called kittens.

Dd

D is for Dinosaur.
Dinosaurs lived millions of years ago. Today scientists dig for their bones to show in museums.

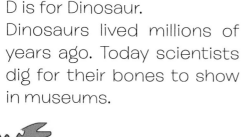

Ee

E is for Elephant.
Elephants are one of the largest animals on our planet. Their very large ears keep them cool. A baby elephant is a calf.

Ff

F is for Fish.
Fishes live in rivers, ponds, lakes and the ocean. Fishes are also kept as pets in aquariums.

Gg

G is for Goat.
Goats are farm animals. Goats are kept by many people for their milk and meat. Baby goats are called kids.

Hh

H is for Hippopotamus. Hippopotamuses are large animals that live in Africa. They spent their days in water to keep cool. At nights they eat grass. A group of hippopotamuses is called a pod. A baby hippopotamus is a calf.

Ii

I is for Iguana.
Iguanas are large lizards that have scales on their bodies. They live in warm places. They eat mainly plants.

Jj

J is for Jaguar.
Jaguars are animals that live in the prairies of Africa. They are from the cat family. They run fast.

Kk

K is for Kangaroo
Kangaroos are found in Australia. They hop and bounce around quickly on two legs. They travel in groups called mobs.

Ll

L is for Lion.
Lions are seen as the king of the African jungle. You can also see lions in zoos in many countries. Baby lions are called cubs.

Mm

M is for Macaws.
Macaws are parrots. These large colorful birds are often kept as pets.

Nn

N is for Newt.
Newts are a kind of salamander. They live on land as well as in water.

Oo

O is for Octopus.
Octopuses live in the ocean. They have eight legs.

Pp

P is for Panda.
Pandas are a kind of bear found in Central China. You can also see them in zoos in other countries.

Qq

Q is for Quail.
Quails are small birds that live in the forests and woodlands all around the world.

Rr

R is for Raccoon
Raccoons are cuddly animals. They are very intelligent and love to climb trees. They eat both plants and animals.

Ss

S is for Seal.
Seals make their homes on land and in cold often frozen waters. Seals have four large flippers instead of feet. Baby seals are called pups.

Tt

T is for Tiger.
Tigers are large animals of the cat family. They live in different types of places in the world such as forests, grasslands and wetlands. Tigers' furs are orange and black stripes. The babies are called cubs.

Uu

U is for Umbrella Bird.
Umbrella Birds are large birds that live in the rain forests of Central and South America. The Umbrella Bird has a large crest on top of its head.

Vv

V is for Vulture.
Vultures are birds of prey. Vultures keep the environment clean by eating dead animals.

Ww

W is for Wolf.
Wolves are wild dogs. They are good hunters.
They live in groups called packs.

Xx

X is for X-ray Fish
This small freshwater fish has its spine
and insides showing like an x-ray.

Yy

Y is for Yak.
Yaks look like cows. In some countries they are used by farmers to pull heavy loads.

Zz

Z s for Zebra.
Zebras are in the horse family. They have their own pattern of stripes. They stick together in groups called a herd. Grass is their main food.

Do you know your letters?

Q E V e k X W R w f o D
Q N v p E K C M J A R z
Y u a D I B Z H O t S T c
G F u x C V N B q F G A
M H n z S L Y D b A r l j
I j H O M q w l A D f d h
Z X L x n r g Q P K E l b R
A o g H T s q h l R l J k m
P Q r a x M l e b p Y m B
K I G j R Z f H R z g l j Z T
F W r w x p G a D B p v U

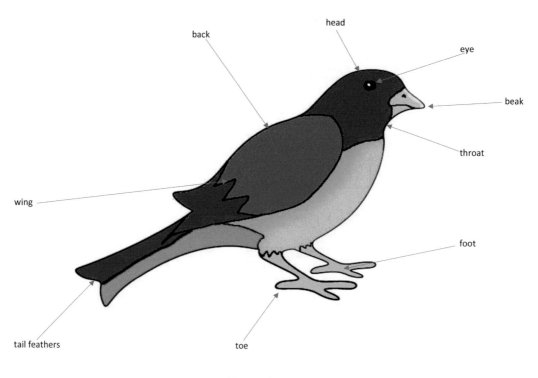

back
head
eye
beak
throat
wing
foot
tail feathers
toe

Bird Facts

A bird is a mammal because they are warm-blooded. The two distinctive characteristics of birds are, they have feathers and wings. Birds fly by flapping their wings and using air pressure to lift them. Feathers are important to birds because they keep them warm and help them to operate. Some bird's feathers provide camouflage. For example, a parakeet can hide among the branches of a green tree and not seen.

Although one of the main characteristics of birds is they can fly, not all birds can fly. Penguins, Kiwis, and Ostriches cannot fly. However, although they cannot fly, penguins are excellent swimmers and ostriches fast runners.

Different kinds of birds eat different types of things. Some birds eat insects, fruits, seeds, small animals, fish. Vultures eat dead animals.

People keep some birds such as parrots, canaries, finches, cockatiels as pets.

Most baby birds are chicks. Some baby birds have a particular name; for example, a baby duck is a duckling, a baby goose is a gosling.

The scientists who study birds is an ornithologist.

Parts of a Fish

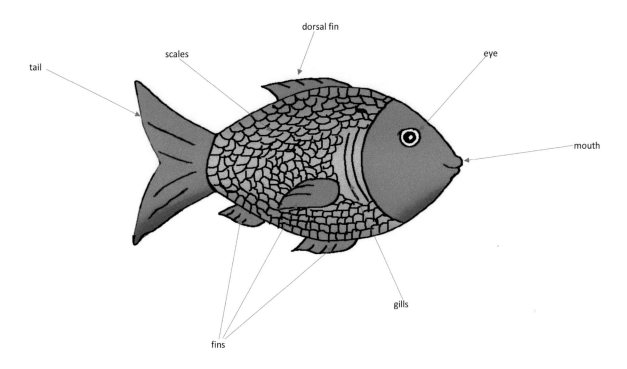

Fish Facts

A fish is an animal that lives and breathes in water. They breathe through gills and have scales. There are many species of fish, the largest being the Great Whale Shark. All fish are vertebrates and are coldblooded. Coldblooded means animals whose body temperature varies with that of their surroundings. For example, fishes that live in a lake during the Spring and Summer will not die if the lake freezes during the winter because their body will adjust to the cold. Fish eat other fish, aquatic plants, and planktons. Some fish live in freshwaters, such as lakes, rivers, and ponds, others in the ocean. A group of fish is a school.

Scientists who study fish is an ichthyologist.

Sight Words

is	where	often	some
for	there	the	over
in	many	these	give
and	make	found	could
they	good	other	away
other	eat	find	every
their	show	live	only
out	our	black	must
of	have	such	into
come	from	large	help
are	around	keep	from
that	also	look	said
like	what	some	seen

Homes are great places for children to learn to read, write and have fun.

A Note for Parents

Families play a significant role in the development of every aspect of a child's physical, emotional and intellectual development. The home is often described as the first learning environment for children. One simple way to help children excel in kindergarten is to expose them to the Alphabet and other learning materials before they begin kindergarten. Research has shown exposing children to books and other reading materials build their literacy skills.

This book is specifically written to support the needs of the Kindergarten child and First Graders who are struggling with learning to read. The child's ability to read and write depends on their understanding of letters and letter sounds.

Learning the Alphabet is the foundation to learn to read and write, therefore parents should include the Alphabet in the collection of materials they choose to help the child learn at home. Researchers have agreed that knowing the Alphabet at the entry of Kindergarten is one of the strongest predictors of success in reading during the First Grade, therefore children must be given all possible exposures to the letters of the Alphabet and the sounds of these letters in order to learn to read.

As a teacher of Kindergarten children, I believe an Alphabet book must do more than teach the alphabet. It must expose children to some high frequency words that they are expected to know in Kindergarten, build vocabulary and give information. High frequency words are words that appear often in printed text.

For example *the, like, we, she, eat* are a few of those words.

In the State of Georgia, for example, Bibb County Schools require their kindergartners to know at least 100 high frequency words (sight words) before First Grade. Teachers usually push for students to learn more because the more they know the more likely it is for them to succeed in reading. First Grade has their own set of high-frequency words that students are expected to know before they go to the Second Grade.

My Animal Alphabet does not only teach the alphabet, but it gives facts on each animal. This child friendly information includes many high frequency words that children can learn while learning the Alphabet. Parents must initially read the book to the child and it is simple enough for the child to read on their own after their parents have read it to them a few times.

The aim of this book is to prepare the young child for Kindergarten literacy, and give them a strong foundation to succeed as they move through the other grades. My hope is that parents and children will enjoy every part of it.

About the Author:

Delores Henriques began her training to be an educator at age eighteen. As long as she could remember she wanted to be An educator. At this point she has earned a B.A. in Education from the University of the West Indies, M.Ed. from the American InterContinental University and her Ed.S. in Early Childhood Education from North Central University.

Her philosophy "Every child can learn" gives her the strong conviction to support the individual needs of the children she teaches. Her knowledge that children learn in different ways, and implementing strategies to support the individual needs of the students, has given her the opportunity to see her students grow, and succeed in all areas of learning and development.

She believes the goal of Early Childhood Education is to get young children to read, write, think, and reason. Her desire is to help each young child achieve these goals.

She is married with two adult children and six grandchildren.

Printed in the United States
By Bookmasters